Street by Street

SOUTHPORT

FORMBY, ORMSKIRK, SKELMERSDALE

Ainsdale, Aughton Park, Banks, Bescar, Birkdale, Burscough, Churchtown, Hightown, Scarisbrick, Up Holland

1st edition April 2002

© Automobile Association Developments Limited 2002

Ordnance Survey®   This product includes map data licensed from Ordnance Survey® with the permission of the Controller of Her Majesty's Stationery Office. © Crown copyright 2002. All rights reserved. Licence No: 399221.

All rights reserved. No part of this publication may be reproduced, stored in a retrieval system, or transmitted in any form or by any means– electronic, mechanical, photocopying, recording or otherwise – unless the permission of the publisher has been given beforehand.

Published by AA Publishing (a trading name of Automobile Association Developments Limited, whose registered office is Millstream, Maidenhead Road, Windsor, Berkshire SL4 5GD. Registered number 1878835).

The Post Office is a registered trademark of Post Office Ltd. in the UK and other countries.

Mapping produced by the Cartographic Department of The Automobile Association. A00965

A CIP Catalogue record for this book is available from the British Library.

Printed by GRAFIASA S.A., Porto Portugal.

The contents of this atlas are believed to be correct at the time of the latest revision. However, the publishers cannot be held responsible for loss occasioned to any person acting or refraining from action as a result of any material in this atlas, nor for any errors, omissions or changes in such material. The publishers would welcome information to correct any errors or omissions and to keep this atlas up to date. Please write to Publishing, The Automobile Association, Fanum House (FH17), Basing View, Basingstoke, Hampshire, RG21 4EA.

Ref: ML202

ii

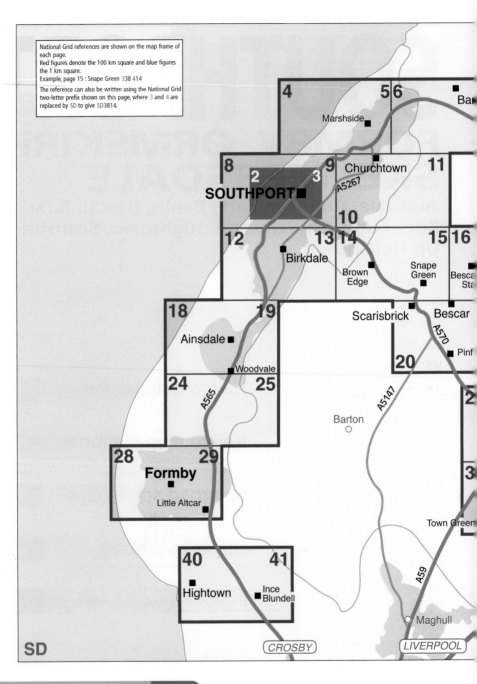

National Grid references are shown on the map frame of each page.
Red figures denote the 100 km square and blue figures the 1 km square.
Example, page 15 : Snape Green 338 414

The reference can also be written using the National Grid two-letter prefix shown on this page, where 3 and 4 are replaced by SD to give SD3814.

4

Marshside ∎

5 6

Ba

8

2

3 9

Churchtown

SOUTHPORT ∎

A5267

11

10

12

13 14

Birkdale

Brown Edge

15 16

Snape Green

Besca Sta

18

19

Ainsdale ∎

Scarisbrick

Bescar

A570

20

Pinf

Woodvale ∎

24

A565

25

Barton ○

A5147

2

28

29

Formby ∎

Little Altcar ∎

3

Town Green

40

41

Hightown ∎

Ince Blundell ∎

A59

Maghull ○

SD

CROSBY

LIVERPOOL

Enlarged scale pages 1:10,000 6.3 inches to 1 mile

0 1/4 miles 1/2

0 1/4 1/2 kilometres 3/4 1

PRESTON

A59

Tarleton ○

A565

PRESTON

Leyland ○

SD

A6

A581

CHORLEY

Eccleston ○

Rufford ○

A59

S

Coppull ○

M6

A49

17

23

Burscough ■

A5209

27

Standish ○

27

mskirk

31

A577

on

32

Ashurst ■ **33** **34**

Roby Mill ■

35

Pennylands ■

Skelmersdale

36

4

A570

3

M58

37 **38**

5

Up Holland ■

Orrell ■

39

6/26

A577

Wigan ○

A571

ST HELENS

WARRINGTON

4.2 inches to 1 mile   **Scale of main map pages** 1:15,000

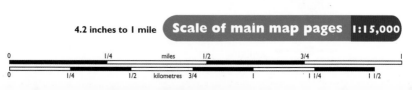

0   1/4   miles   1/2   3/4   1
0   1/4   1/2   kilometres 3/4   1   1 1/4   1 1/2

iv

Junction 9	Motorway & junction	⊖	Underground station
Services	Motorway service area	⊖	Light Railway & station
	Primary road single/dual carriageway	+++++++++	Preserved private railway
Services	Primary road service area	*LC*	Level crossing
	A road single/dual carriageway	●—●—●—●	Tramway
	B road single/dual carriageway	- - - - - - -	Ferry route
	Other road single/dual carriageway	··············	Airport runway
	Minor/private road, access may be restricted	– · — · — · –	Boundaries - borough/district
← ←	One-way street	ᴡᴡᴡᴡᴡᴡᴡ	Mounds
	Pedestrian area	**93**	Page continuation 1:15,000
=============	Track or footpath	**7**	Page continuation to enlarged scale 1:10,000
	Road under construction		River/canal, lake, pier
⊦ – – = = ⊣	Road tunnel		Aqueduct, lock, weir
AA	AA Service Centre	465 ▲ Winter Hill	Peak (with height in metres)
P	Parking		Beach
P+🚌	Park & Ride		Coniferous woodland
🚌	Bus/Coach station		Broadleaved woodland
	Railway & main railway station		Mixed woodland
	Railway & minor railway station		Park

Cemetery		Theme Park	
Built-up area		Abbey, cathedral or priory	
Featured building		Castle	
City wall		Historic house or building	
A&E 24-hour Accident & Emergency hospital		Wakehurst Place NT National Trust property	
PO Post Office		Museum or art gallery	
Public library		Roman antiquity	
i Tourist Information Centre		Ancient site, battlefield or monument	
Petrol station Major suppliers only		Industrial interest	
† Church/chapel		Garden	
Toilet		Arboretum	
Toilet with disabled facilities		Farm or animal centre	
PH Public house AA recommended		Zoological or wildlife collection	
Restaurant AA inspected		Bird collection	
Theatre or performing arts centre		Nature reserve	
Cinema		Visitor or heritage centre	
Golf course		Country park	
▲ Camping AA inspected		Cave	
Caravan Site AA inspected		Windmill	
Camping & Caravan Site AA inspected		Distillery, brewery or vineyard	

2

A　B　8　C　D　E

Southport
Pier

33 2　18　33

SOUTHPORT

1

2

Marine Drive

3

P

Marine Dr

Pleasureland

Southport Zoo &
Conservation
Trust

8

P

Esplanade

4

Marine Drive

Victoria Way

Southport
Swimming
Baths

417

Superstore

PO

Esplanade

P+

Southport
Flower
Show Site

Duke St

Beach Priory Gdns

Hotel

5

Rotten Row

Beach Priory Gdns

Priory Mews

LORD ST WEST

Beechfield Gdns

A565

Beechfield Gdns

Sunnymede
School

Castle Walk

6

Esplanade

Beach Rd

Westcliffe Road

Works

Southern Road

St Paul's

AUGHTON RD

Rotten Row

Twistfield Close

7

Southport
Landing Area

Blandford
Close

Palatine
Road

Gloucester

ROAD

Warren Ct

Weld

Amberley
Close

Ascot Cl

Westcliffe Road

KILWORTH

Saxon

Road

33 2　33

A　B　8　C　D　E

Ascot Cl

I grid square represents 250 metres

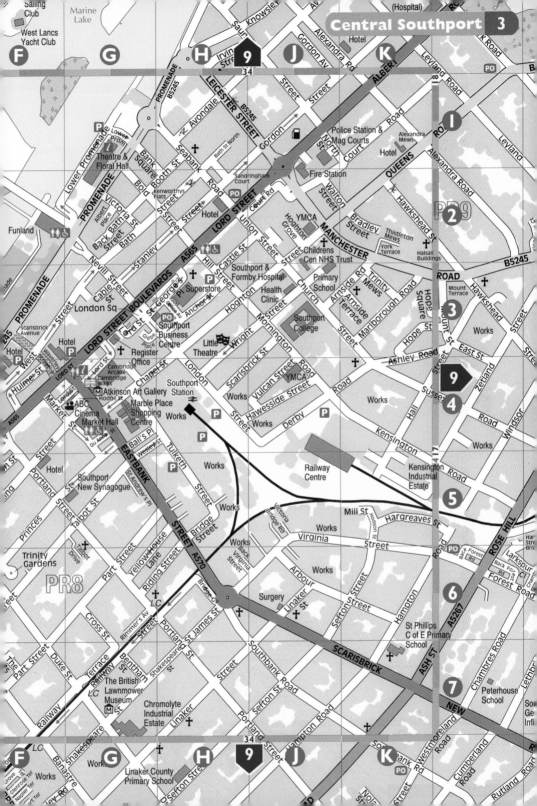

4

A   B   C   D

3 33   34
21

I

2

20   Marshside
Sands

3

419

4

5

Marine Drive

P

3 33   34
A   B   **9**   C   D

Golf Course

Fleetwood

Hesketh Road

Road

Southport
Municipal
Golf Club

Cliff Rd

PA

T ROAD

Fairway

Pro

Albany Road

Leyland
Road

Lathom
Road

Avondale Road

Park Road
West

Hesketh
Centre

Stutelea

Marine Lake

P

Southport
Sailing

I grid square represents 500 metres
Southport

E F G H

36

Crossens
Marsh

I

Works

Crossens
Way

Treen
Close

Kingston Crs

Norbury Rd

Fylde Lane

2

Menivate
Close
Preston
Cl

Glencoyne
Drive

Truro
Dr

Dawlish
Dr

Millar's
Place

Seaton
Way

Northam
Close

Torcross
Close

Salcombe
Dr

Sladburn
Crescent

Mill Cl

Ex Cl

Millar's
Av

Bodmin
Avenue

Crediton
Av

Melrose
Avenue

Eamont
Avenue

Norbury Rd

Fylde Lane

Talaton
Cl

Ottery Close

Salwick
Close

Pilling
Close

Tornes
Drive

Inskip

Works

Seacroft
Crescent

Fylde Road

Merepark
Drive

The

Wo

Rid

Prescall Cl

Elswick Road

Carstang Rd

Freckleton
Road

Hornby
Road

Seaton
Wy

Coyford Dr

Slaidburn

Slaidburn
Industrial Estate

Fylde Road
Industrial
Estate

Glenpark
Drive

Poolside Walk

Holmdale
Av

Douc

3

Caton
Close

Fylde

St Annes
Road

Manx
Jane's
La

Ansdell
GV

Lytham
Road

Kirkham

Road

Road

Fairhaven
Road

Lane

Glenpark
Drive

NEW

Crossns

North

Asland
Garden

Ribble
Avenue

Roselea
Drive

Road

Works

Stanley
High School

St Michael's Cl

Fleetwood
Road

Willowhey

Shellfield
Road

Cleveleys Road

Cleveleys
Avenue

Larkfield

Glamis
Drive

PO

ROAD

Rathmore Crescent

6

Marshside

Road

Paul's
Lane

Granby
Close
Lane

Knob Hall
Lane

Knob Hall
Gdns

Croston's Brow

PO

Walro
Mews

Prestfield
School

Peterhouse
School

PRESTON

Lexton
Drive

4

Works

Fleetwood

Links Avenue

Radnor
Cl

Denbigh
Cl

Eden
Cl

Longacre

Baker's
Lane

The
Ridings

Larkfield
CP School

Mallee
Crs

Mallee
Avenue

Highfield Rd

Balmoral

Merlewood
Av

BANKFIELD LANE

Verulam

RI

Hesketh
Golf Club

Bellis
Av

Threlfalls
Lane

Churchill Avenue

Emmanuel Rd

Cambridge
Gdns

Drive

Baker's Lane

Marshside
Rd

St Patricks
Primary
School

A565

Churchtown
Medical Centre

Churchtown
County Junior
& Infant School

St Cuthbert's
Road

Verulam

B5244

Works

5

Cockle Dick's La

The
Lawns

Br Av

Cambridge Av

Sunny Road

Sally's La

M

Botanic Gardens
Museum

Cockle
Dick's
Lane

Tower Dene
Preparatory School

Beresford
Gardens

Denmark Rd

CAMBRIDGE

ROAD

MANOR

CAMBRIDGE
RD

Ely
MS

BOTANIC

ROAD

Hesketh Road

Allerton Rd

Coudray

Hilbre Rd

Silverthorne
Drive

Beresford Rd

Kings Hey Dr

Montrose Drive

Cooke Drive

Bibby

St Clair
Drive

Church Road

Peet's
Lane

A567

MILL

Off Botanic
Road

H

le
Lane

37

36

10

E F G

Churchtown

Meol's Hall

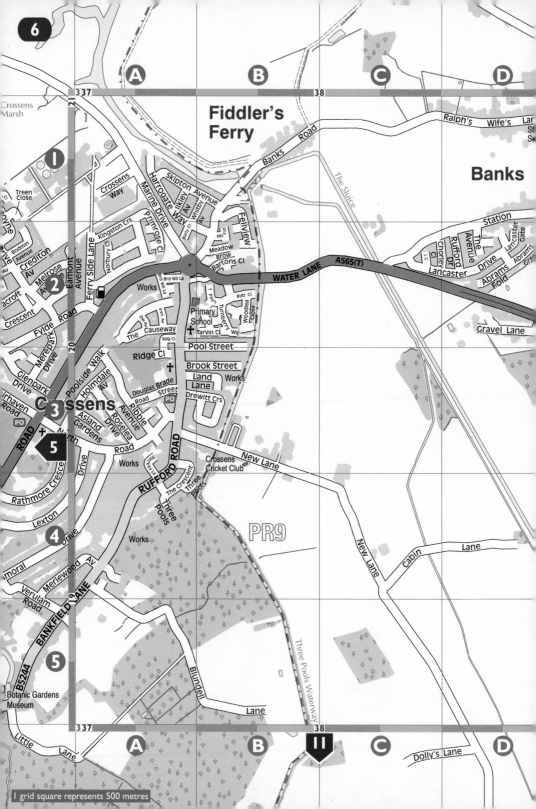

331
32

A B C D

1

18

2

SOUTHPO

Southpo
Pier

3

17

Southport
Flower Show ●
Site

Pleasureland

Espla

Marine
Drive

Victoria
Way

Marine
Drive

P

P

P+🚌

4

Marine
Drive

Esplanade

Southport
Landing Area

Sunnymede
School

Row

Beach
Rd

Rotten

Road

5

Blandford
Close

Warren
Ct

Westcliffe

Palatine
Road

2

X

416
331

Camberley Cl
Palace Road

Ascot
Close

Weld

Grovewood

Saxon Roa

LULWORTH ROAD

Road

Prince Charles G

RNIB
Sunshine
House School

A

B

32

C

D

12

Westbourne
Gardens

Windsor
court

Oxford
Gardens

Oxford
Road

Carnoustie
Cl

Priory
Gardens

Victoria
court

Canterbury
Cl

Westbourne

Regen

Ch
Clo

Three Pools W

Blundell

E F **6** G H
38 39

Dolly's Lane

New Lane

I

Lane

Dolly's Lane

Long Meanygate

Winacre
Farm

2

Moss Lane

Wyke Wood Lane

Straight Up La

Moss Lane

Wyke Hey
Farm

Wyke Lane

3

17

Wyke House
Farm

4

Perch Pool Lane

Wyke Lane

The

Avenue

5

416

Wyke Thorn
Farm

E **15** G H
38 39

Wyke

Pool Lane

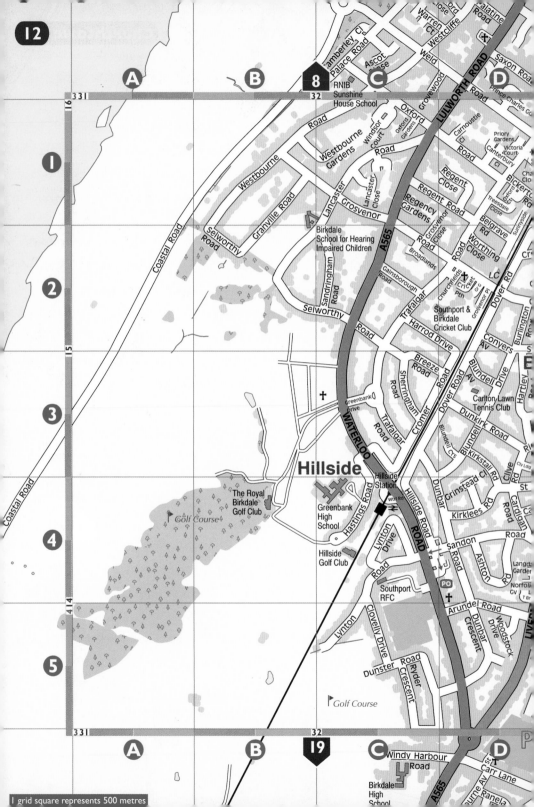

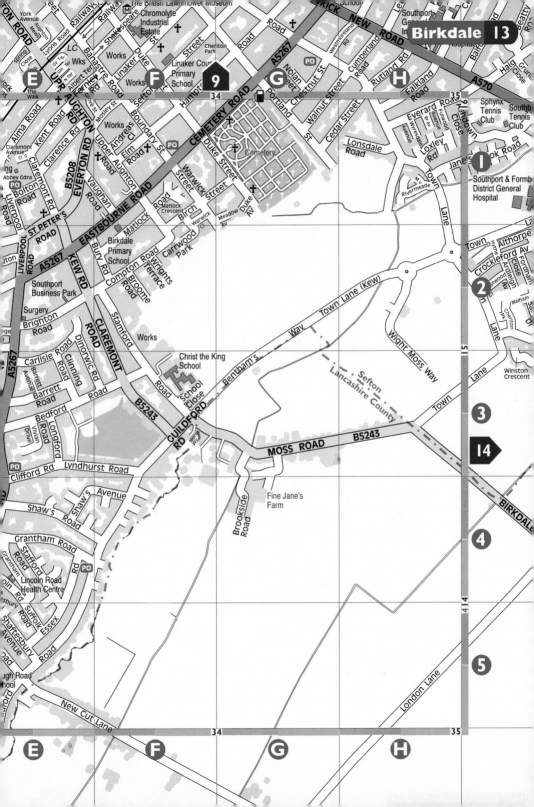

Avenue

A   B   C   D

339   40

16

Midge Hall
Farms

1

Wyke Wood Lane

2

Greenings Lane

15

Greenings

3

15

Perch   Pool   Lane   Bescar   Lane

Midge Hall Lane

Wholesome Lane

PO

Bescar Lane Station

Woodmoss Lane

LC

4

Drummersdale   Lane

White House Lane

414

Copelands

5

Bescar Lane

Hillcrest
Drive

339   40

A   B   21   C   D

Bescar

Culshaw
Wy

Hillock Lane

Hillock Close

Highfield Lane

Everard
Close

Bsc Brw La

Clive's
Farm

dale Lane

B5242

1 grid square represents 500 metres

Canygate

Whams
Farm

E **F** **G** **H**

42 43

Berry House

Berry House Road

I

Windmill
Farm

Wholesome Lane

Fish Lane

2

15

3

Wildfowl and
Wetlands Trust
Martin Mere

4

41.4

LC

5

Martin Lane

LC

42 43

E **F** **G** **H**

New
Lane

Marsh
Moss House

Marsh Moss Lane

Ainsdale-on-Sea

Ainsdale
Sand Dunes

24

Woo

Willowbank H
Home & Tour

1 grid square represents 500 metres

Dunster Road
Ryder Crescent

Golf Course

PR8

Farnborough Road Junior School
Central Avenue
Guildford

E F 12 G H

32 33

Windy Harbour Road
St Mary's Gdns
Carr Lane
Leybourne Av
Ranelagh Dr

Birkdale High School

A565

Nixon's Lane

Birkdale Cemetery

Philip Drive

Charles Av
Anne Av
Mary Av
Elizabeth Av

ROAD

Welwyn Avenue

Ainsdale High School

Birkdale RC Cemetery

Heathfield Road

George Drive

Southport & Ainsdale Golf Club

Bradshaw's Lane

Berwick Av

Carlton Road
Sandringham Road

Faulkner Cl

LIVERPOOL

Fairfield Road

Road

Burnley

Oakwood Av
Oakwood Drive

PO

Mill Road

Moss View

Ainsdale Station
Station

PO
Surgery

Rd

Sanvino Avenue

Leamington Road
Liverpool Rd

Segar's Lane

Limont Rd

Halifax Road

Ainsdale

Salford

Greenford Road
Trevor Rd
Stourton Rd

Road

Fraley Close
Stoneleigh Close

Kenilworth

Road

Wentworth Close

Eldons Cft

Unit Road

Sandbrook Road

Ainsdale C of E Primary School

Staveley Rd

Orchard Lane
Briar Rd
Sandbrook Rd

Hill House Farm

Orchard Lane

White Otter Farm

Segar's Lane

Headbolt

12

11

32 33

Bowness Av

Keswick Close

Ainsdale Clinic

Woodvale CP Sch

Kings Meadow

PO

Sandbrook Road

Meadow

Meadow Lane

Heather Rd
Lilac Av
Cherry Road

St John Stone Primary School

Woodvale Road

Rose Crs

A565

OOL ROAD

E F 25 G H

32 33

1
2
3
4
5

20

20

ACKSMERE

A LANE

337

B Marks School

15

38

C Sandy Brook

D

Woodland Avenue

Hill Dri

Scarisbrick

B5242

1

Hooton's Farm

13

Bullens Lane

A570(T)

BESCAR BROW LANE

SOUTHPORT ROAD

Mancha

2

Black

Moss Lane

3

Police Station

Renacres Hall Hospital

2

Renacres Lane

A5147

A570(T)

4

GORSUCH LANE

SOUTHPORT ROAD

Pinfo

Halsall Moss

5

A5147

Morris HeV

Morris Lane

Leeds & Liverpool Canal

Pinfold Lane

S Ch

Gre 337 Lane

A

337

ROAD

B

38

Small Lane North

C

D

Hulmes Bridge Business Centre

North Moor

Grange

I grid square represents 500 metres

E F **16** G H

40 41

Bescar

Hillock Lane
Hillock Close
Hall Road
HALL

nersdale

Scarisbrick
Hall

ROAD

Highfield Lane

Drummersdale Lane

I

13

2

Merscar Lane

3

DAM WOOD LANE

12

Leeds & Liverpool Canal

Shaw Hall
Caravan Park

**Heatons
Bridge**

4

Smithy Lane

HEATONS BRIDGE ROAD

**Hurlston
Green**

Moorfield La

5

Moorfield

B5242

Lan41

A E T) SOUTHPORT

E F G H

40 41

Hurlston Hall
Golf Club

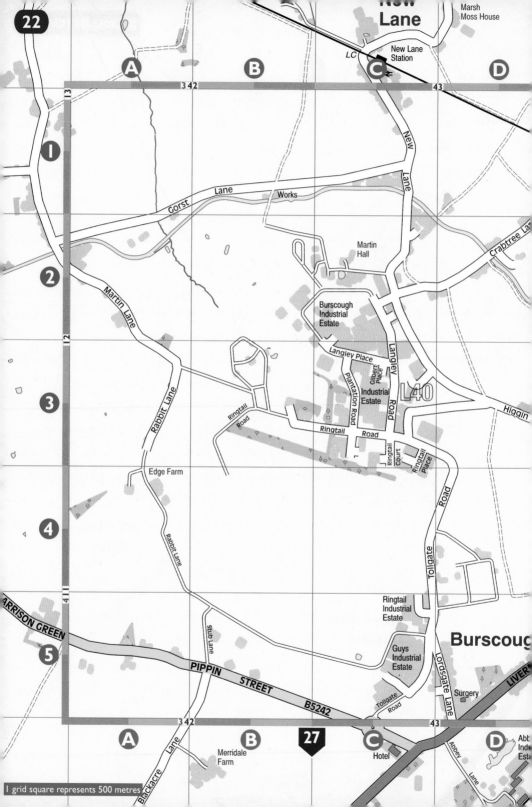

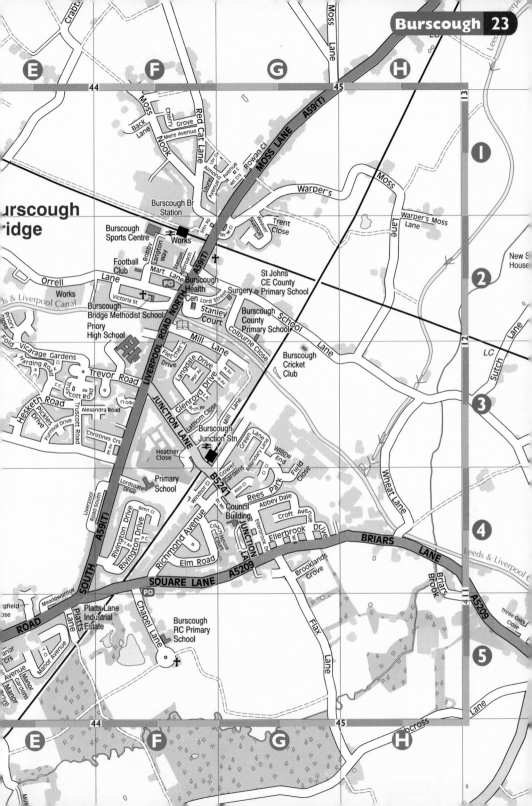

A   B   C   D

3 40   41

I

Diglake
Farm

Jackson's

Common
Lane

Lane

Hurlston Hall
Golf Club

Hurlston Lane

Hurlston
Lane

Hurlston Hall
Country Caravan Park

MOSS LANE

ARROW

2

Spout
House Farm

A570(T)

SOUTHPORT

Heskin
Hall

Heskin Lane

Marians Drive

Ren
Clos

Rutland Crs

Ludlow

Haslam Drive

Douglas
Drive

West End
County Primary
School

3

Asmall
House

Blindman's Lane

Lane

ROAD

Courtfield

Fairfield
Close

Grimshaw

Highfield Road

Crgm

Fr'd Dr

Alx Ms

4

Asmall
Lane

Asmall
CP School

Whiterails
Ms

Wrls Cl

Tennyson Drive

Whiterails
Drive

Cotton Drive

Halsall Lane

Asmall
Close

The Reeds

Church Road

Cottage Lane

Kinloch Way

County

ROAD

SOUTHPORT RD

Ormskirk
RUFC

Works

Civic Hall

Church Fields

Rothwell
Close

Green

The Avenue

Rose Croft

Pe
Av

Han
Lan

5

Redgate

Cottage Ms

Ash
Close

Beechwood
Drive

Oak
Ave

Redgate

Foxwood Drive

Holborn Hill

Garnett
Gdns

Cottage
Lane

The Birch

County
Primary
Sch

Kingsbury
Sch

Vicarage
Walk

Park
Pool

P   P

P

Superstore

CHURCH ST

A570(T)

AUGHTON ST

3 40   41

A   B   **30**   C   D

St Bedes
RC School

A59(T)

AUGHTON
ST

ANNE'S ROAD

Dyer's Lane

Brook Farm

Moorgate

Bridge
Path

PIPPIN STREET

E   F   **22**   G   H

42   43

Club Lane

Guys Industrial Estate

Lordsgate Lane

Gollgate Road

Surgery

Hotel

LIVERP

Manor Avenue

Dam Close

Mill Dam Lane

Manor Gardens

Manor Drive

Blackacre Lane

Merridale Farm

Abbey Lane

Abbey Lane Industrial Estate

Mill Dam Lane

I

Abbey Lane

Abbey Farm Caravan Park

2

HIGH LANE

Mawdsley Terrace

Dawson Road

Tyrer Road

Sephton Drive

Scott Drive

arroll Crescent

rescent

cent

A59(T)

Dark Lane

Sandy Lane

3

Lathom Lane

Lady's Walk

BURSCOUGH ROAD

B5319

Gr Pk

Pine CV

Pine Avenue

Old Boundary Way

Brooklands

Pine

Works

Works

Tree Road

ncroft

Crft Av

Ln Rd

Dark Lane

Bath Farm

Dark Lane

4

Waterworks House

Waterworks Road

Nursery Avenue

Greetby Hill

Greetbye

Pendle Dr

Ormskirk Business Park

Hardacre Street

New Court Way

Greetby Hill CE Junior School

Greetby

5

To DI

Charlesbye Av

Field Walk

P

Ormskirk Station

Bath Springs

Register Office

Mag

Railway Rd

Surgery

Derby Street

Derby Hill Road

Thompson

Edgley Drive

Taylor Avenue

Latham Avenue

Field Walk

Lady's Walk

P

P

Council Building

Sunnyfields

Tower

Hill

E   **F**   **31**   **G**   **H**

WIGAN ROAD

A&E

PO

Ormskirk & District

Ormskirk General Hospital

Cross Hall High School

CROSSHALL BROW

A577

408

KNOWSLEY ROAD

A570(T)

Windmill Av

Mill

Ormskirk Grammar School

School House

42   43

all Brow Clos

Beech Meadow

Weldon Drive

Ruff Lane

Milton Drive

Normanhurst

rlgowrle

ns

Small Lane

OOR ST

A50(T)

ORD

AD

ORMSKIRK

Wes

3 27   28

A **B** **C** **D**

1

2

3

4

5

08

07

06

Golf Course

Formby
Formby La
Golf Club

Shireburn Road

Freshfield

Fairways Court
Badgers Rake
Tower End

Victoria Road

Victoria Road

squirrel Green

Firs
Firs Cl
Firs Crs
Firs Link

Birch Green

Proctor Road

Gorse W.

St Peter's Way
Oakfield Drive
Larch Avenue
College Close
St Peter's Close

Harington

Holmwood Dr

Avenue

Dunes Drive

Larkhill

Blundell Avenue

Lane

Wicks Crs

Wicks Green
Wicks Green Close

Warren Gn

Ince Crs

Harington Close

Green

Barkfield Road

Weld Dr

Holmwood

Beech Dr

PO

Harington Gn

Wicks Crs

Harington Lane

Wicks Dri Cl

St Jeromes
RC Primary
School

Spruce Way

Edenhurst Dr

Greenloon's

Foxhill

Greenloon's Walk

Greenloon's Drive

Kirklake Bank

Edenhurst Cl

Archway

Ormins Dr

St Georges Cl

Grnins Dr

Woodlands
Primary
School

Grasmere

Derwent Avenue

Coniston Road

Langdale

Wol Ci
Mere Rd

Woodlands Road

Kirklake Road

St Luke's Drive

Church Walk

Church Way

St
Luke's
Drive

Bushby's Park

Bushby's Lane

Brooks Way

Brooks Road

Spruce Way

Lifeboat Road

Shorrocks Hill
Country Club

Lime Tree Way

Trap Hill

Maple Close

St Lukes C of E
Primary School

Pinewood Close

Elm Drive

Pinewood Avenue

Beechwood Way
Ash Grove
Cedar Grove
Sycamore Grove
Aspen Gv
Milford Cl

Chestnut Drive

Cambridge Rd

Heydon Close

Mayfield Av

Hadstock Avenue

Jubilee Avenue

Funchal Av

Road

Tadlow Close
Meldreth Close
Burwell Avenue
Orwell

Stapleton Road

Sealand Cl

Elsworth Cl

Alexandra Road

Albert Road

Road

A **B** **C** **D**

Range
High
School

3 27   28

4 06

4 07

1 grid square represents 500 metres

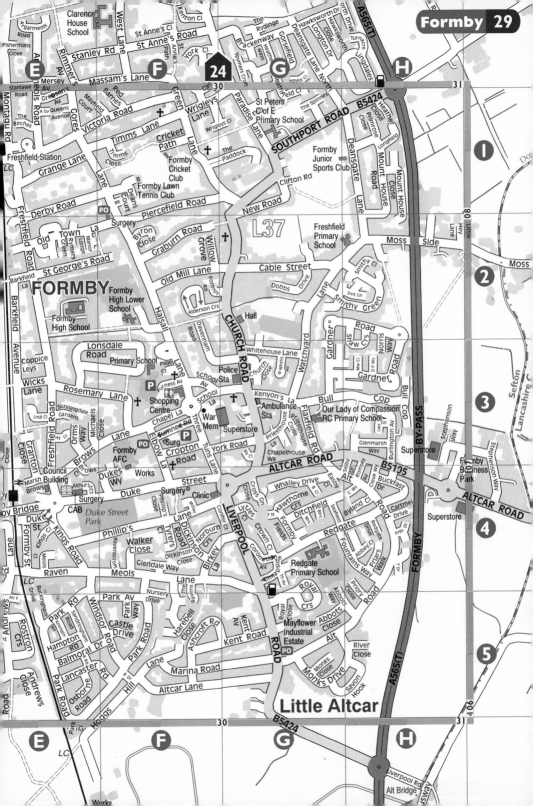

Surgery
Derby street
Council Building
sunnyfields
Edgley Drive
Derby Hill Road
Abbotsford
Taylor
Avenue
Latham Avenue
Tower

WIGAN ROAD
A50(T)

Windmill Av
Mill Street
School Lane

E
A5
KNOWSLEY ROAD

F
A&E
Ormskirk &
District
Ormskirk & District
General Hospital
Ormskirk Grammar School

42

27

Cross High
School

G

Hall Brow Close

Lady's Walk

H

43
A577 CROSSHALL BROW

08

ORMSKIRK

I

We

Ruff
Farm

Small
Lane

Ormskirk
Cricket
Club

Weldon
Drive

Blairgowrie
Gardens

Ruff Lane
Milton Drive
Normanhurst
Beech Meadow
Woodlands Close

SAINT

Edge Hill
University
College

The
Sporting
Edge Track

Ruff Lane

Vicarage
Close

St James
Close

Bewcastle Dr

Varlian
Close

2
Vicarage Lane

07

Altys Lane

HELENS

Slack House
Farm

ROAD

A570(T)

Scarth Hill Lane

Wellfield Lane

Whiteley's Lane

3

Scarth Hill

Works

Catharine's
Lane

Cropper's   Lane

Poppy Lane

Poppy Lane

4

406

5

Clock House

Moss
End

ORMSKIRK ROAD

Lane

High

E   **F**   **G**   **H**

42   43

Long Lane

A   B   C   D

3 46   47   08

I

Spa Lane

Holland
Business
Park   Spa
Farm

Spa Lane

Cock Farm

Firswood Road

07

2

Stanley
Place
Seaton
Place

Way

Stanle

Works

Seddon Place

Statham Road

Staveley Road

Works

Selby Place

Slate

Lane

Chapel House

Works

NEVERSTITCH ROAD

Thurcroft Dr

Mealby
Close

Tintagel

Tiverton Av

Old Engine Lane

3

A577

BLAGUEGATE LANE

ORMSKIRK   ROAD

Turnberry

Black Moss
Special
School

Brookfield
CP School

Kinsbury
School

Tongbarn

Kiln

Tilcroft

Palm

School Lane

Back
School
Lane

Victoria
Pk

Clayton Street

Council
Building

4

406

Holland's

Lane

Blaguegate

Bromilow Road

Orm
Works

Taylor St

Witham
Road

Marchbank
Road

Sandy Lane

Sherrat Street

Oxford St

Laburnum
Dr

Ash Grove

Olive Gv

Cambridge Rd

Lancaster Crescent

Lilac Grove

Rose Crs

Cedar Gv

Oak Ct s

Lime Grove

Skelmersdale
Park CP
School

Fern
Close

Hawthor

Pennylands

Primary
School

PO

Sandy
Lane
Health Cen

Smith
St

Barnes Road

Waverley

Westgate

Birch Grove

Ann Street

Whitener

Westock

Street

5

Kerfoots
Lane

Liverpool Road

RAILWAY RD

Council
Building High

Ashwall
Street

Wallcroft
Street

Wheatacre

Whitney
Road

LIVERPOOL RD

Derby
Rd

Skelmersdale
United FC

Old Town
Cl

Old Town Wy

Village Cl

Westgate

B5312

RAILWAY ROAD

Gladden Place

Gardine
Place

A   B   36   C   D

3 46   M58   47

ERSDALE ROAD B5312

White   Road

White Mo

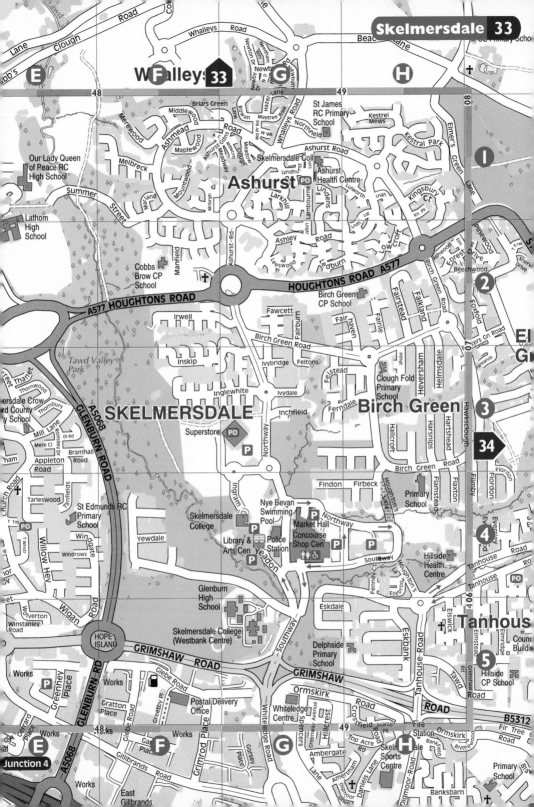

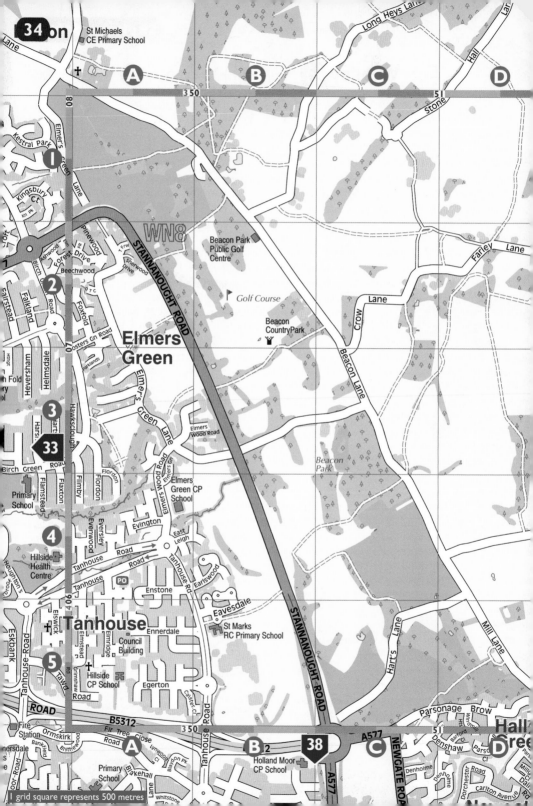

St Michaels
CE Primary School

A **B** **C** **D**

80 3 50 51 Stone

Long Heys Lane

Hall

Lane

Kestral Park

I

Kingsbury
Ct

Kn Pk

Elmer's Green Lane

WN8

Pinewood

Forest Drive

Beechwood

Sherwood
Drive

Beacon Park
Public Golf
Centre

Farley Lane

2

Birch

Falkland

Road

Fairstead

Foxfold

osters on Road

Golf Course

Crow Lane

Beacon Lane

**Elmers
Green**

Beacon
CountryPark

Heversham

Helmsdale

Hawksclough

Elmer's Green Lane

Elmers
Wood Road

3

33

Hart

Harsl

Birch Green

Road

Flimby

Flordon

Flordon

Elmers Wood Road

Elmers Gn

Beacon
Park

Primary
School

Flamstead

Flaxton

Eversley

Evenwood

Evington

Elmers
Green CP
School

4

Hillside
Health
Centre

Houghton's

Tanhouse   Road

East
Leigh

Tanhouse Rd

Earlswood

Tanhouse   Road

PO

Enstone

Eavesdale

Tanhouse

Eskbank

Tanhouse Road

Elswick

Tawd Road

Ennerdale

Council
Building

Elmstead

Elmridge

5

Hillside
CP School

Grimshaw Road

Egerton

St Marks
RC Primary School

Hart's Lane

Mill Lane

ROAD

B5312 3 50 51

Parsonage Brow

Denshaw

Hall
Gree

Fire
Station

Ormskirk

Fir Tree Close

Lynwood

Road

Blythfield

Blakehall

whitstone

Lane

A **B** 2 **38** **C** A577 **D**

Holland Moor
CP School

A577

NEWGATE ROAD

Denholme

Dorchester
Road

Carlton Avenue

Primary
School

STANNANOUGHT ROAD

1 grid square represents 500 metres

Holland Lees

Forest Fold Farm

Golf Course

E **F** **G** **H**

52 53 08

Ba

Bank Road

Brow

Bank Top

Ayrefield Lane

I

Roby Mill

Cemetery

Roby Mill CE Sch

School Lane

2 **Gat**

Dean Wood

oby ill

PO

Latford Lane

Stoney Brow

3

St Josephs RC College

Whitley Road

Dean Wood Av

Cathurst Road

GATHURST

ROAD

M6

107

St Theresa's School

College Road

Lafford Lane

Golf Course

Dean Wood Golf Club

Spring Road

Eton Way

Derwent Road

Coniston Road

Oxford Rd

406

4

5

Hallbridge Gardens

DINGLE ROAD A577

Dingle Av

Hillgate

Woodside Cl

GROVE ROAD

PARLIAMENT STREET

Grasmere

52 53

E **F** ▼ **39** **G** **H**

Primary School

Surgery

Priory Rd

Orrell Post

Ullswater Av

Thames Dr

St Pete RC Hig

PO

Hall Green

Abbey Close

Windermere Rd

36

A · B · 32 · C · D

LIVERPOOL RD
RAILWAY ROAD
B5312
Gladden Place
Cardine place
Westgate
Street Wallcroft Street
Wheatacre
Old Town
Derby Rd
...rsdale
...FC Old Town Wy
Kerfoots Lane

3 46 · 47

White Moss Road

M58

SKELMERSDALE ROAD B5312

I

White Mo...

Stanley Farm

05

M58

2

Rainford Road

A570(T)

3

04

4

Coal Pit Lane

Holly Lane

5

Holly Fold Farm

News Lane

403

Ben Lane Farm
Ben Lane Court

3 46 · 47

A · B · C · D

Park

1 grid square represents 500 metres

E F G H

I

32 33 05

The Wi

Mic

Withins Lane

Lower

Car

Monks

Carr

Lane

River Alt

2

04

3

Lancashire County
Sefton

Lady
Green

House   Lane

Carr

Hall

Lane

Carr
Houses

Blackcar

Lane

Marsh
Lane

Lady Green Lane

The
Cross

Moor Lane

The Close

Victoria Road

Victoria Rd

Ince
Blundell

Back o The Town

Carr Side Lane

Carr Side
Farm

4

403

A565(T)

Cross Barn Lane

Lane

Park Wall Road

5

East La

MOOR

LANE

Moss
Wood

Wall

Road

32 33

E F G H

USING THE STREET INDEX

Street names are listed alphabetically. Each street name is followed by its postal town or area locality, the Postcode District, the page number, and the reference to the square in which the name is found.

Standard index entries are shown as follows:

Abbey Cl *FMBY* L37 ....**29** H4

Street names and selected addresses not shown on the map due to scale restrictions are shown in the index with an asterisk or with the name of an adjoining road in brackets:

Admiralty Cl *BRSC* * L40 ....**22** D5

Bank Nook
CHTN/BK (off Radnor Dr) PR9 ....**5** F4

GENERAL ABBREVIATIONS

ACC	ACCESS	E	EAST	LDG	LODGE	R	ROUNDA
ALY	ALLEY	EMB	EMBANKMENT	LGT	LIGHT	RBT	
AP	APPROACH	EMBY	EMBASSY	LK	LOCK	RD	
AR	ARCADE	ESP	ESPLANADE	LKS	LAKES	RDG	
ASS	ASSOCIATION	EST	ESTATE	LNDG	LANDING	REP	REF
AV	AVENUE	EX	EXCHANGE	LTL	LITTLE	RES	RESE
BCH	BEACH	EXPY	EXPRESSWAY	LWR	LOWER	RFC	RUGBY FOOTBALL
BLDS	BUILDINGS	EXT	EXTENSION	MAG	MAGISTRATE	RI	
BND	BEND	F/O	FLYOVER	MAN	MANSIONS	RP	
BNK	BANK	FC	FOOTBALL CLUB	MD	MEAD	RW	
BR	BRIDGE	FK	FORK	MDW	MEADOWS	S	
BRK	BROOK	FLD	FIELD	MEM	MEMORIAL	SCH	SC
BTM	BOTTOM	FLDS	FIELDS	MKT	MARKET	SE	SOUTH
BUS	BUSINESS	FLS	FALLS	MKTS	MARKETS	SER	SERVICE
BVD	BOULEVARD	FLS	FLATS	ML	MALL	SH	
BY	BYPASS	FM	FARM	ML	MILL	SHOP	SHO
CATH	CATHEDRAL	FT	FORT	MNR	MANOR	SKWY	S
CEM	CEMETERY	FWY	FREEWAY	MS	MEWS	SMT	S
CEN	CENTRE	FY	FERRY	MSN	MISSION	SOC	SC
CFT	CROFT	GA	GATE	MT	MOUNT	SP	
CH	CHURCH	GAL	GALLERY	MTN	MOUNTAIN	SPR	S
CHA	CHASE	GDN	GARDEN	MTS	MOUNTAINS	SQ	SC
CHYD	CHURCHYARD	GDNS	GARDENS	MUS	MUSEUM	ST	S
CIR	CIRCLE	GLD	GLADE	MWY	MOTORWAY	STN	ST
CIRC	CIRCUS	GLN	GLEN	N	NORTH	STR	ST
CL	CLOSE	GN	GREEN	NE	NORTH EAST	STRD	
CLFS	CLIFFS	GND	GROUND	NW	NORTH WEST	SW	SOUTH
CMP	CAMP	GRA	GRANGE	O/P	OVERPASS	TDG	TR
CNR	CORNER	GRG	GARAGE	OFF	OFFICE	TER	TE
CO	COUNTY	GT	GREAT	ORCH	ORCHARD	THWY	THROU
COLL	COLLEGE	GTWY	GATEWAY	OV	OVAL	TNL	T
COM	COMMON	GV	GROVE	PAL	PALACE	TOLL	TO
COMM	COMMISSION	HGR	HIGHER	PAS	PASSAGE	TPK	TUR
CON	CONVENT	HL	HILL	PAV	PAVILION	TR	
COT	COTTAGE	HLS	HILLS	PDE	PARADE	TRL	
COTS	COTTAGES	HO	HOUSE	PH	PUBLIC HOUSE	TWR	
CP	CAPE	HOL	HOLLOW	PK	PARK	U/P	UNDE
CPS	COPSE	HOSP	HOSPITAL	PKWY	PARKWAY	UNI	UNIV
CR	CREEK	HRB	HARBOUR	PL	PLACE	UPR	
CREM	CREMATORIUM	HTH	HEATH	PLN	PLAIN	V	
CRS	CRESCENT	HTS	HEIGHTS	PLNS	PLAINS	VA	
CSWY	CAUSEWAY	HVN	HAVEN	PLZ	PLAZA	VIAD	VI
CT	COURT	HWY	HIGHWAY	POL	POLICE STATION	VIL	
CTRL	CENTRAL	IMP	IMPERIAL	PR	PRINCE	VIS	
CTS	COURTS	IN	INLET	PREC	PRECINCT	VLG	V
CTYD	COURTYARD	IND EST	INDUSTRIAL ESTATE	PREP	PREPARATORY	VLS	
CUTT	CUTTINGS	INF	INFIRMARY	PRIM	PRIMARY	VW	
CV	COVE	INFO	INFORMATION	PROM	PROMENADE	W	
CYN	CANYON	INT	INTERCHANGE	PRS	PRINCESS	WD	
DEPT	DEPARTMENT	IS	ISLAND	PRT	PORT	WHF	
DL	DALE	JCT	JUNCTION	PT	POINT	WK	
DM	DAM	JTY	JETTY	PTH	PATH	WKS	
DR	DRIVE	KG	KING	PZ	PIAZZA	WLS	
DRO	DROVE	KNL	KNOLL	QD	QUADRANT	WY	
DRY	DRIVEWAY	L	LAKE	QU	QUEEN	YD	
DWGS	DWELLINGS	LA	LANE	QY	QUAY	YHA	YOUTH

POSTCODE TOWNS AND AREA ABBREVIATIONS

BRSC	Burscough	KIRK/FR/WAR	Kirkham/Freckleton/	SFTN	Sefton	WGNNW/ST	Wigan north
CHTN/BK	Churchtown/Banks		Warton	SKEL	Skelmersdale		S
FMBY	Formby	ORM	Ormskirk	STHP	Southport	WGNW/BIL/OR	Wigan west/B
HTWN	Hightown	RNFD/HAY	Rainford/Haydock				

.a FMBY L37 29 E1
.eld FMBY L37 24 C5
Wy FMBY L37 28 C2
Pl SKEL WN8 37 G1
a CHTN/BK PR9 22 A1
h La BRSC L40 20 B4
th Rd CHTN/BK PR9 10 B2
Gdns BRSC L40 23 G4
n Rd FMBY L37 29 F2
n Dr STHP PR8 18 C3
/ Cl CHTN/BK PR9 5 F4
e Av CHTN/BK PR9 10 A2
e La FMBY L37 29 E1
e Rd CHTN/BK PR9 10 A3
am Cl STHP PR8 13 E4
am Rd STHP PR8 13 E4
n Cl FMBY L37 29 E3
lle Cl ORM L39 30 A4
lle Pk ORM L39 30 B5
lle Pk West ORM L39 30 A5
le Rd STHP PR8 12 B2
ere Av SKEL WN8 35 E5
ere Rd FMBY L37 28 D3
n Pl SKEL WN8 33 F5
La CHTN/BK PR9 7 E3
s Cl CHTN/BK PR9 7 E2
s Hall Av CHTN/BK PR9 7 E2
bank ORM L39 30 B3
bank Av
W/BIL/O WN5 39 G5
bank Dr STHP PR8 12 C3
ield Rd STHP PR8 15 E4
ord Cl WGNW/BIL/O WN5 39 G2
ord Rd STHP PR8 19 E4
ey Pl SKEL WN8 33 E5
ngs La CHTN/BK PR9 16 C2
La BRSC L40 23 G3
/BK PR9 7 G3
/ L37 24 B5
L39 26 D4
W/BIL/O WN5 39 G5
Lane Av ORM * L39 26 D4
ea Cl WGNW/BIL/O WN5 39 G3
oon's Dr FMBY L37 28 C3
oon's Wk FMBY L37 28 C4
late Ct
W/BIL/O WN5 39 G5
late Rd
W/BIL/O WN5 39 H5
Wk STHP PR8 19 F3
way Av SKEL WN8 37 G1
way Cl SKEL WN8 32 D3
ways WGNW/BIL/O WN5 39 G5
wood Cl ORM L39 30 B4
y Hl ORM L39 27 F5
y Pl SKEL WN8 33 F5
n's Av FMBY L37 29 E1
ars Rd STHP PR8 18 D2
okes ORM L39 30 C3
ns Dr CHTN/BK PR9 10 B2
d Pl SKEL WN8 37 F1
aw La ORM L39 26 D4
aw Rd SKEL WN8 34 A5
ead Cl STHP PR8 12 D4
ale Cl FMBY L37 29 E3
enor Cl STHP PR8 12 C2
enor Gdns STHP PR8 12 D2
enor Pl STHP PR8 12 D2
enor Rd STHP PR8 12 C1
Pk CHTN/BK PR9 10 B1
L39 27 E3
Rd SKEL WN8 35 E5
St STHP PR8 9 E5
Ter STHP PR8 9 E5
wood STHP PR8 12 C1
/ Cl STHP PR8 10 A5
ord Rd STHP PR8 13 E5
Hall La CHTN/BK PR9 7 E2

H

ock Av FMBY L37 28 D5
v STHP PR8 10 A5
Rd STHP PR8 19 E3
dge Gdns SKEL WN8 35 E5
ow Cl BRSC L40 31 G1
ft SKEL WN8 33 H3
SKEL WN8 39 E1
een Cl SKEL WN8 39 E1
HTWN L38 41 G3
or Cl ORM L39 30 C3
BRSC L40 21 F1
CHTN/BK PR9 3 K4
Buildings CHTN/BK PR9 3 K2
La FMBY L37 29 F2
L39 26 C4
Rd STHP PR8 13 E5
ton Rd FMBY L37 29 E5
PR8 3 K6
ock WGNW/BIL/O WN5 39 H3
La ORM L39 26 D4
y Av STHP PR8 18 C4
cre St ORM L39 27 E4
g Rd BRSC L40 23 E3
ell Cl FMBY L37 29 F5
La STHP PR8 15 F4
ood Av STHP PR8 19 E2
Hargreaves St STHP PR8 3 K5
Harington Cl FMBY L37 28 D3
Harington Gn FMBY L37 28 D3
Harington Rd FMBY L37 28 C2
Harrod Dr STHP PR8 12 C2
Harrogate Wy CHTN/BK PR9 6 A1
Harsnips SKEL WN8 33 H3
Hartland Av CHTN/BK PR9 5 H2
Hartley Crs STHP PR8 12 D3
Hartley Rd STHP PR8 12 D3
Hartshead SKEL WN8 33 H3
Hart's La SKEL WN8 34 C5
Hart St STHP PR8 9 H4
Hart Street Br CHTN/BK PR9 9 H4
Hartwood Rd CHTN/BK PR9 9 H2
Harvington Dr STHP PR8 18 C3
Haslam Dr ORM L39 26 C3
Hastings Rd STHP PR8 12 C4
Hatfield Rd STHP PR8 19 E2
Haven Brow ORM L39 30 B5
Hawesside St CHTN/BK PR9 3 H4
Hawksclough SKEL WN8 33 H3
Hawkshead St CHTN/BK PR9 3 K2
Hawksworth Cl FMBY L37 24 C5
Hawksworth Dr FMBY L37 24 C5
Hawthorn Crs SKEL WN8 32 D4
Hawthorne Crs FMBY L37 29 G4
Hawthorne Gv CHTN/BK PR9 10 B3
Hayfield Rd ORM L39 26 D3
Hazelbank Gdns
FMBY (off Freshfield Rd) L37 29 E1
Hazel Gv STHP PR8 10 A3
Hazel La SKEL WN8 33 G1
Hazelwood Av BRSC L40 23 F3
Hazlehurst Cl FMBY L37 28 C4
Heanor Dr STHP PR8 14 B2
Heather Cl BRSC L40 23 F3
FMBY L37 29 H1
STHP PR8 25 F1
Heatherlea Cl SKEL WN8 39 F1
Heatherways FMBY L37 24 C5
Heathey La STHP PR8 14 B5
Heathfield Cl FMBY L37 24 C5
Heathfield Rd STHP PR8 19 G3
Heathgate SKEL WN8 33 H3
Heaton Cl BRSC L40 23 E3
SKEL WN8 38 D1
Heatons Bridge Rd BRSC L40 21 H4
Helmsdale SKEL WN8 33 H3
Helston Cl CHTN/BK PR9 5 H2
Henley Dr CHTN/BK PR9 10 A1
Hereford Rd CHTN/BK PR9 10 B3
Hesketh Av CHTN/BK PR9 7 E1
Hesketh Dr CHTN/BK PR9 5 E5
Hesketh Rd BRSC L40 23 E3
CHTN/BK PR9 4 D4
Heskin La ORM L39 26 C2
Hester Cl HTWN L38 40 A3
Heversham SKEL WN8 33 H3
Heydon Cl FMBY L37 28 D5
Heyes Rd WGNW/BIL/O WN5 39 H2
Heysham Rd CHTN/BK PR9 10 B3
Heywood Cl FMBY L37 29 E3
Higgin's La BRSC L40 22 D3
Higher La SKEL WN8 39 F1
Higher Vw SKEL WN8 39 F2
Highfield La BRSC L40 21 G1
Highfield Rd CHTN/BK PR9 5 H4
ORM L39 26 D4
Highgate Rd SKEL WN8 39 E1
High La BRSC L40 27 F2
ORM L39 31 H5
Highmeadow SKEL WN8 38 D1
High Moss ORM L39 30 D2
High Park Pl CHTN/BK PR9 10 C2
High Park Rd CHTN/BK PR9 10 C2
High St SKEL WN8 32 D4
Hilbre Cl CHTN/BK PR9 10 A1
Hillcrest SKEL WN8 37 G1
Hillcrest Dr BRSC L40 15 H5
Hillcrest Rd ORM L39 26 D4
Hilldean SKEL WN8 35 F5
Hillock Cl BRSC L40 21 E1
Hillock La BRSC L40 21 E1
Hillside Av ORM L39 30 C1
Hillside Rd STHP PR8 12 C4
Hill St CHTN/BK PR9 3 H2
Hillsview Rd STHP PR8 19 E4
Hilltop Wk ORM L39 30 B2
Hodge St STHP PR8 3 G4
Hodson St STHP PR8 3 K5
Hoghton Gv CHTN/BK PR9 3 J2
Hoghton St CHTN/BK PR9 3 H3
Holborn Dr ORM L39 30 B2
Holborn Hl ORM L39 30 B2
Holgate Dr WGNW/BIL/O WN5 39 H3
Holland Moss SKEL WN8 37 F3
Hollybrook Rd STHP PR8 2 E7
Holly Cl SKEL WN8 32 D4
Holly Fold La RNFD/HAY WA11 36 D5
Holly La ORM L39 30 A1
SKEL WN8 36 C4
Holmdale Av CHTN/BK PR9 6 A3
Holmfield Pk FMBY L37 28 D2
Holmwood Cl FMBY L37 28 D3
Holmwood Dr FMBY L37 28 D2
Holmwood Gdns FMBY L37 28 D2
Holt St WGNW/BIL/O WN5 39 G3
Hoole La CHTN/BK PR9 7 E1
Hope Island SKEL WN8 33 E5
Hope Sq CHTN/BK PR9 3 K3
Hope St CHTN/BK PR9 3 K3
Hornby Rd CHTN/BK PR9 5 G3
Houghton's La SKEL WN8 33 H4
Houghtons Rd SKEL WN8 33 F2
Hulme St STHP PR8 3 F4
Huntingdon Ct
CHTN/BK (off Manor Rd) PR9 5 G5
Hurlston Av SKEL * WN8 33 H5
Hurlston Dr ORM L39 26 D3
Hurlston La BRSC L40 26 B1
Hutton Ct SKEL WN8 32 C4
Hutton Rd SKEL WN8 32 C4
Hutton Wy ORM L39 26 D5
Hythe Cl STHP PR8 14 A2

I

Ilkley Av CHTN/BK PR9 6 A1
Ince Crs FMBY L37 28 D3
Inchfield SKEL WN8 33 G3
Ingleton Rd STHP PR8 14 A2
Inglewhite SKEL WN8 33 F3
Ingram SKEL WN8 33 G4
Inskip SKEL WN8 33 F3
Inskip Rd CHTN/BK PR9 5 G3
Irton Rd CHTN/BK PR9 10 A2
Irvin Av CHTN/BK PR9 6 A2
Irving St CHTN/BK PR9 9 F1
Irwell SKEL WN8 33 F2
Ivybridge SKEL WN8 33 G3
Ivydale SKEL WN8 33 G3
Ivy St STHP PR8 9 H4

J

Jacksmere La BRSC L40 14 D5
Jane's Brook Rd STHP PR8 13 H1
Jubilee Av ORM L39 27 E4
WGNW/BIL/O WN5 39 G4
Jubilee Dr SKEL WN8 32 D5
Jubilee Rd FMBY L37 28 D5
Junction La BRSC L40 23 G4

K

Keats Ter STHP PR8 10 B4
Kempton Park Fold STHP PR8 14 B2
Kendal Wy STHP PR8 18 D5
Kenilworth Rd STHP PR8 19 E4
Kensington Rd CHTN/BK PR9 3 K4
FMBY L37 29 E5
Kent Av FMBY L37 29 G5
Kenton Cl FMBY L37 24 B5
Kent Rd FMBY L37 29 G5
STHP PR8 13 E1
Kenworthys Flats CHTN/BK PR9 3 G2
Kenyon's La FMBY L37 29 G3
Kerfoot's La SKEL WN8 32 B5
Kerslake Wy HTWN L38 40 A3
Kerton Rw
STHP (off Bickerton Rd) PR8 12 D1
Kestral Pk SKEL WN8 33 H1
Kestrel Ms SKEL WN8 33 H1
Keswick Cl STHP PR8 19 E5
Kettering Rd STHP PR8 18 D3
Kew Rd FMBY L37 28 D5
STHP PR8 13 E2
Kilburn Rd SKEL WN8 39 F3
Killingbeck Cl BRSC L40 23 E3
Kiln La SKEL WN8 32 D3
Kingfisher Ct CHTN/BK PR9 9 H2
Kingfisher Pk SKEL WN8 33 H1
Kingsbury Cl STHP PR8 18 C4
Kingsbury Ct SKEL WN8 33 H1
Kings Cl FMBY L37 29 E4
Kings Hey Dr CHTN/BK PR9 10 B1
Kings Meadow STHP PR8 19 F5
Kings Rd FMBY L37 29 E4
Kingston Crs CHTN/BK PR9 6 A2
King St STHP PR8 3 F5
Kingsway STHP PR8 2 E4
Kinloch Wy ORM L39 26 C5
Kirkdale Gdns SKEL * WN8 38 C1
Kirkham Rd CHTN/BK PR9 5 G3
Kirklake Bank FMBY L37 28 C4
Kirklake Rd FMBY L37 28 C4
Kirklees Rd STHP PR8 12 D4
Kirkstall Dr FMBY L37 29 H4
Kirkstall Rd STHP PR8 12 D3
Knob Hall Gdns CHTN/BK PR9 5 F4
Knob Hall La CHTN/BK PR9 5 F4
Knowle Av STHP PR8 19 E2
Knowsley Rd CHTN/BK PR9 9 F1
ORM L39 27 E5

L

Laburnum Dr SKEL WN8 32 C4
Laburnum Gv BRSC L40 23 F1
STHP PR8 10 B3
Lady Green Cl HTWN * L38 41 F4
Lady Green La HTWN L38 41 E3
Lady's Wk BRSC L40 27 G5
Lafford La SKEL WN8 35 F2
Lakes Dr WGNW/BIL/O WN5 39 H2
Lakeside Av WGNW/BIL/O WN5 39 H5
Lakeside Ct
STHP (off Prom) PR8 3 G2
Lambourne SKEL WN8 33 G1
Lancaster Cl STHP PR8 12 C1
Lancaster Crs SKEL WN8 32 D4
Lancaster Dr CHTN/BK PR9 6 C2
Lancaster Ga CHTN/BK PR9 6 D2
Lancaster Rd FMBY L37 29 E5
STHP PR8 12 C1
Land La CHTN/BK PR9 6 A3
Langdale Av FMBY L37 28 D3
Langdale Cl FMBY L37 28 D4
Langdale Dr BRSC L40 23 F3
Langdale Gdns STHP PR8 12 D4
Langley Cl HTWN L38 40 A5
Langley Pl BRSC L40 22 C3
Langley Rd BRSC L40 22 C3
Langtree SKEL WN8 33 G2
Lansdowne Rd STHP PR8 10 A4
Larch Cl SKEL WN8 32 D4
Larch St STHP PR8 10 A5
Larch Wy FMBY L37 28 D2
Larkfield La CHTN/BK PR9 5 G4
Larkhill SKEL WN8 33 G1
Larkhill Gv HTWN L38 40 A4
Larkhill La FMBY L37 28 C2
Larkspur Cl STHP PR8 9 H4
Latham Av ORM L39 27 F5
Lathom Cl BRSC L40 23 F3
Lathom La BRSC L40 27 H3
Lathom Rd CHTN/BK PR9 9 G1
Laurel Av BRSC L40 23 F1
Laurel Dr SKEL WN8 32 D3
Laurel Gv CHTN/BK PR9 10 A3
Lawns Av SKEL WN8 39 F3
The Lawns CHTN/BK PR9 5 F5
Lawson St CHTN/BK PR9 10 C3
Lea Crs ORM L39 26 D3
Leamington Rd STHP PR8 19 E3
Ledburn SKEL WN8 33 G2
Leeswood SKEL WN8 33 G2
Leicester St CHTN/BK PR9 3 H1
Lendel Cl FMBY L37 29 E3
Lenton Av FMBY L37 28 D2
Lesley Rd STHP PR8 10 A3
Lethbridge Rd STHP PR8 9 H5
Levens Cl CHTN/BK PR9 7 E2
Lexton Dr CHTN/BK PR9 5 H4
Leybourne Av STHP PR8 19 H1
Leyland Cl CHTN/BK PR9 6 C2
Leyland Rd CHTN/BK PR9 9 G1
STHP PR8 9 G1
Leyland Wy ORM L39 27 E5
Lifeboat Rd FMBY L37 28 A5
Lighthorne Dr STHP PR8 18 C4
Lilac Av STHP PR8 25 F1
Lilac Gv SKEL WN8 32 D4
Limefield Dr SKEL WN8 38 B1
Lime Gv SKEL WN8 32 D4
Lime St STHP PR8 10 A4
Lime Tree Wy FMBY L37 28 C4
Limont Rd STHP PR8 19 F3
Linaker St STHP PR8 3 H7
Lincoln Rd STHP PR8 13 E4
Linden Av WGNW/BIL/O WN5 39 H2
Linden Gv WGNW/BIL/O WN5 39 H2
Lindens SKEL WN8 33 G1
Lindholme SKEL WN8 33 H2
Lindley Av WGNW/BIL/O WN5 39 F3
Lingdales FMBY L37 24 D5
Links Av CHTN/BK PR9 5 E5
Little Hey La FMBY L37 29 H2
Little La CHTN/BK PR9 10 D1
Liverpool Av STHP PR8 19 F3
Liverpool Old Rd STHP PR8 25 E2
Liverpool Rd FMBY L37 29 G4
ORM L39 30 A3
SKEL WN8 32 C5
STHP PR8 25 E1
Liverpool Rd North BRSC L40 23 F3
Liverpool Rd South BRSC L40 23 E4
Lodge Rd WGNW/BIL/O WN5 39 H4
London La STHP PR8 13 H5
London Sq STHP PR8 3 G3
London St CHTN/BK PR9 3 H4
Longacre CHTN/BK PR9 5 F4
Longcliffe Dr STHP PR8 18 D4
Longfield FMBY L37 29 H1
Longford Rd STHP PR8 13 E3
Longhey SKEL WN8 33 H1
Long La CHTN/BK PR9 7 F1
ORM L39 30 C3
SKEL WN8 38 B5
Long Meanygate CHTN/BK PR9 11 H2
Longton Dr FMBY L37 24 C5
Lonsdale Av ORM L39 27 E3
Lonsdale Rd FMBY L37 29 E3
STHP PR8 13 H1
Lordsgate Dr BRSC L40 23 F4
Lordsgate La BRSC L40 22 C5
Lord St BRSC L40 23 F2
CHTN/BK PR9 3 H2

Gv ORM L39 .... 30 C1
Ms STHP PR8 .... 2 D5
Nook SKEL WN8 .... 39 F1
Rd SKEL WN8 .... 39 F1
t Rd CHTN/BK PR9 .... 28 C2
nade STHP PR8 .... 3 F3
PR8 .... 18 B2
ct Pl SKEL WN8 .... 38 C3

Q

Dr ORM L39 .... 30 B4
Mt ORM L39 .... 27 F4
Anne St STHP PR8 .... 3 E4
s Av FMBY L37 .... 29 E1
s Cft FMBY L37 .... 28 D4
s Rd CHTN/BK PR9 .... 5 K2
L37 .... 28 D4
PR8 .... 18 B2
St ORM L39 .... 30 D1
n Cl STHP PR8 .... 18 C4

R

La BRSC L40 .... 22 A4
Dr CHTN/BK PR9 .... 5 F4
Ap ORM L39 .... 27 E5
Pth ORM L39 .... 30 D1
Rd SKEL WN8 .... 32 C5
t STHP PR8 .... 3 G7
Ter STHP PR8 .... 3 F7
d Rd ORM L39 .... 36 B4
Wife's La CHTN/BK PR9 .... 6 D1
hr Dr STHP PR8 .... 19 H1
ne Rd HTWN L38 .... 40 A3
ore Crs CHTN/BK PR9 .... 5 H4
ead Dr SKEL WN8 .... 38 C2
ead Wy SKEL WN8 .... 38 C2
Meols La FMBY L37 .... 29 E4
croft FMBY L37 .... 29 F4
croft Av ORM L39 .... 30 D1
ens FMBY L37 .... 29 F4
son Ct
/BK
awlinson Rd) PR9 .... 9 H2
son Rd CHTN/BK PR9 .... 10 A1
y Rd CHTN/BK PR9 .... 10 B1
rnes FMBY L37 .... 24 B5
Cl FMBY PR8 .... 14 B2
fe Gdns ORM L39 .... 30 D2
ld ORM L39 .... 30 B3
e FMBY L37 .... 29 G4
L39 .... 30 C1
se Dr FMBY L37 .... 29 H4
s Dr STHP PR8 .... 14 B2
nds ORM L39 .... 30 C2
od Dr ORM L39 .... 30 C1
eds ORM L39 .... 26 C1
k BRSC L40 .... 23 G4
y Gdns STHP PR8 .... 12 C1
Cl STHP PR8 .... 12 C1
s Fld
y Cl ORM (off Victoria Rd) L37 .... 28 D1
Av CHTN/BK PR9 .... 6 A3
ond Av BRSC L40 .... 23 F4
ond Ct HTWN L38 .... 40 A5
ond Ms BRSC L40 .... 23 F4
ond Rd STHP PR8 .... 12 D5
Cl CHTN/BK PR9 .... 6 A2
dings CHTN/BK PR9 .... 5 G4
St STHP PR8 .... 3 G6
er Gn STHP PR8 .... 15 F4
y Av FMBY L37 .... 24 A5
PR8 .... 3 G6
Cl BRSC L40 .... 22 C3
l Pl BRSC L40 .... 22 C4
l Rd BRSC L40 .... 22 B3
l STHP PR8 .... 14 B2
l FMBY L37 .... 29 H1
eade STHP PR8 .... 13 H1
le HTWN L38 .... 40 A3
St WGNW/BIL/O WN5 .... 39 H2
on Cl STHP PR8 .... 13 E2
on Dr BRSC L40 .... 23 F4
PR8 .... 39 F1
l SKEL WN8 .... 35 D2
PR9 .... 10 A2
rk Ms CHTN/BK PR9 .... 9 H4
y Dr SKEL WN8 .... 33 E3
y Dr SKEL WN8 .... 29 H4
ry Rd CHTN/BK PR9 .... 10 A1
ay CHTN/BK PR9 .... 29 G3
ery St STHP PR8 .... 10 C4
r SKEL WN8 .... 32 D4
PR8 .... 25 E1
oft Cl ORM L39 .... 26 D4
l STHP PR8 .... 9 H4
l Dr ORM L39 .... 30 B3
a Dr CHTN/BK PR9 .... 6 A3
ary La FMBY L37 .... 29 E3
l ORM L39 ....

Rostron Crs FMBY L37 .... 29 E5
Rothley Av STHP PR8 .... 18 C4
Rothwell Cl ORM L39 .... 26 C5
Rothwell Dr ORM L39 .... 30 A3
Rotten Rw STHP PR8 .... 2 B7
The Roundway HTWN L38 .... 40 A4
Rowan Av BRSC L40 .... 23 G4
Rowan La SKEL WN8 .... 33 C1
Royal Cl FMBY L37 .... 29 G5
Royal Crs FMBY L37 .... 29 G4
Royal Ter STHP PR8 .... 3 F4
Ruddington Rd STHP PR8 .... 14 A3
Ruff La ORM L39 .... 31 F1
Rufford Dr CHTN/BK PR9 .... 6 D2
Rufford Rd CHTN/BK PR9 .... 6 A4
Russell Av CHTN/BK PR9 .... 10 C3
Russell Rd CHTN/BK PR9 .... 10 C3
Rutland Crs ORM L39 .... 26 C3
Rutland Rd STHP PR8 .... 9 H5
Ryburn Rd ORM L39 .... 30 C1
Rydal Av FMBY L37 .... 30 B3
Ryder Cl ORM L39 .... 30 B3
Ryder Crs ORM L39 .... 30 B3
The Rydinge FMBY L37 .... 24 C5
Rymers Gn FMBY L37 .... 29 E2

S

Sagar Fold ORM L39 .... 30 C5
St Andrew's Pl STHP PR8 .... 3 J7
St Anne's Cl FMBY L37 .... 24 B5
St Anne's Rd FMBY L37 .... 24 B5
St Annes Rd CHTN/BK PR9 .... 5 F3
FMBY L37 .... 24 B5
ORM L39 .... 30 C1
St Bedes Cl ORM L39 .... 30 C1
St Clair Dr CHTN/BK PR9 .... 10 C1
St Cuthbert's Rd CHTN/BK PR9 .... 5 H5
St George's Pl STHP PR8 .... 3 G3
St George's Rd FMBY L37 .... 40 A2
HTWN L38 ....
St Helens Rd ORM L39 .... 27 E5
Saint Helens Rd ORM L39 .... 31 E1
St Helens Rd ORM L39 .... 31 C3
St James Cl BRSC L40 .... 31 H2
St James' Rd WGNW/BIL/O WN5 .... 39 G4
St James St STHP PR8 .... 3 H7
St Johns Ct
STHP (off Liverpool Rd) PR8 .... 19 F4
St John's Rd STHP PR8 .... 12 D4
St Luke's Church Rd FMBY L37 .... 28 C4
St Luke's Cl FMBY L37 .... 28 C4
WGNW/BIL/O WN5 .... 39 G4
St Luke's Gv CHTN/BK PR9 .... 10 A3
St Luke's Rd STHP PR8 .... 9 H3
St Mary's Gdns STHP PR8 .... 19 H1
St Michael's Cl CHTN/BK PR9 .... 5 F4
St Paul's Pas STHP PR8 .... 3 F6
St Paul's Sq STHP PR8 .... 2 E6
St Paul's St STHP PR8 .... 3 G6
St Peter's Av FMBY L37 .... 28 D2
St Peter's Cl FMBY L37 .... 28 D2
St Peter's Rd STHP PR8 .... 13 E2
St Stephen's Rd HTWN L38 .... 40 A3
St Thomas's Ct
SKEL (off Church St) WN8 .... 39 F1
St Vincent's Wy STHP PR8 .... 12 D1
Salcombe Dr CHTN/BK PR9 .... 5 G2
Salford Rd STHP PR8 .... 19 E3
Salisbury Rd STHP PR8 .... 10 C4
Sallowfields WGNW/BIL/O WN5 .... 39 G3
Sally's La FMBY L37 .... 5 G5
Salwick Cl CHTN/BK PR9 .... 5 F2
Sambourn Fold STHP PR8 .... 18 C3
Sandbrook Gdns
WGNW/BIL/O WN5 .... 39 G3
Sandbrook Rd STHP PR8 .... 19 E5
WGNW/BIL/O WN5 .... 39 F3
Sandfield Pk ORM L39 .... 30 C3
Sandheys Dr CHTN/BK PR9 .... 10 B1
Sandhills HTWN L38 ....
Sandhurst Cl FMBY L37 .... 28 C5
Sandilands Gv HTWN L38 .... 40 A4
Sandon Rd STHP PR8 .... 12 D4
Sandringham Cl FMBY L37 .... 28 C5
Sandringham Rd CHTN/BK PR9 .... 3 H1
FMBY L37 .... 29 E5
STHP PR8 .... 19 E3
Sandy La HTWN L38 .... 40 A5
SKEL WN8 .... 32 C4
WGNW/BIL/O WN5 .... 39 G4
Sanfield Cl ORM L39 .... 26 C4
Sangness Dr STHP PR8 .... 14 A2
Sanvino Av STHP PR8 .... 19 F3
Saunders St CHTN/BK PR9 .... 9 F1
Savon Hook FMBY L37 .... 29 H5
Sawdon Av STHP PR8 .... 14 A1
Saxon Rd STHP PR8 .... 4 D1
Scaffold La HTWN L38 .... 40 D1
Scarisbrick Av STHP PR8 .... 3 F3
Scarisbrick New Rd STHP PR8 .... 3 J7
Scarisbrick St CHTN/BK PR9 .... 5 F3
ORM L39 .... 26 D4
Scarth Hill La BRSC L40 .... 31 D3
ORM L39 .... 30 D3
Scarth Pk SKEL WN8 .... 37 H1

School Av FMBY L37 .... 29 F3
School Cl ORM * L39 .... 30 B4
STHP PR8 .... 13 F3
School House Gn ORM L39 .... 27 E5
School House Gv BRSC * L40 .... 23 E2
School Houses
SKEL (off Tawd Valley Pk) WN8 .... 33 C5
School La BRSC L40 .... 23 G2
FMBY L37 .... 29 F3
SKEL WN8 .... 32 D5
SKEL WN8 .... 35 G2
SKEL WN8 .... 39 F1
School Rd HTWN L38 .... 40 A3
Schwartzman Dr CHTN/BK PR9 .... 7 E1
Scott Dr ORM L39 .... 30 A3
Scott St CHTN/BK PR9 .... 10 C3
Seabank Rd CHTN/BK PR9 .... 3 J3
Seacroft Crs CHTN/BK PR9 .... 5 G2
Seafield FMBY L37 .... 29 E4
Seafield Rd STHP PR8 .... 19 E2
Sealand Av FMBY L37 .... 28 D4
Sealand Cl FMBY L37 .... 28 D4
Seaton Pl SKEL WN8 .... 32 D2
Seaton Wy CHTN/BK PR9 .... 5 G2
Seddon Pl SKEL WN8 .... 32 D2
Sefton Av WGNW/BIL/O WN5 .... 39 G3
Sefton Cl WGNW/BIL/O WN5 .... 39 G3
Sefton Rd CHTN/BK PR9 .... 29 E4
WGNW/BIL/O WN5 .... 39 G3
Sefton St STHP PR8 .... 3 J6
Sefton Ter WGNW/BIL/O WN5 .... 39 G3
Segar's La STHP PR8 .... 19 F3
Selby Dr FMBY L37 .... 29 H4
Selby Pl SKEL WN8 .... 32 D2
Selworthy Rd STHP PR8 .... 12 B2
Sephton Dr ORM L39 .... 27 E5
The Serpentine ORM L39 .... 30 C5
Sevenoaks Av STHP PR8 .... 18 D3
Shaftesbury Av STHP PR8 .... 13 E5
Shaftesbury Gv STHP PR8 .... 13 E4
Shaftesbury Rd STHP PR8 .... 13 E4
Shakespeare St STHP PR8 .... 3 G3
Shaw Crs FMBY L37 .... 29 H2
Shaw's Av STHP PR8 .... 13 H2
Shaw's Rd STHP PR8 .... 13 H2
Shelley Dr ORM L39 .... 26 C4
Shelley Gv STHP PR8 .... 13 H2
Shellfield Rd CHTN/BK PR9 .... 5 G4
Shelton Dr STHP PR8 .... 18 C4
Shenley Wy CHTN/BK * PR9 .... 5 B2
Sherrat St SKEL WN8 .... 32 C4
Sherringham Rd STHP PR8 .... 12 C5
Sherwood Av ORM L39 .... 30 B3
Sherwood Dr SKEL WN8 .... 34 A2
Shirdley Crs STHP PR8 .... 19 E5
Shireburn Rd FMBY L37 .... 28 C3
Shirewell Rd WGNW/BIL/O WN5 .... 39 H3
Shore Rd STHP PR8 .... 3 F5
Sidney Rd CHTN/BK PR9 .... 10 B1
Silverthorne Dr CHTN/BK PR9 .... 10 B1
Skipton Av CHTN/BK PR9 .... 6 A1
Slackey La CHTN/BK PR9 .... 5 J3
Slaidburn Crs CHTN/BK PR9 .... 5 G2
Slate La SKEL WN8 .... 32 B3
ORM L39 .... 31 E1
Small La BRSC L40 .... 17 E5
Smith St SKEL WN8 .... 32 C4
Smithy Cl CHTN/BK PR9 .... 29 H2
Smithy Gn FMBY L37 .... 29 G2
Smithy La BRSC L40 .... 21 C4
Snape Gn STHP PR8 .... 25 E1
Somerset Dr STHP PR8 .... 25 E1
Southbank Rd STHP PR8 .... 3 H7
Southern Rd STHP PR8 .... 2 E6
Southport New Rd CHTN/BK PR9 .... 7 F3
Southport Old Rd FMBY L37 .... 24 D4
Southport Rd FMBY L37 .... 29 G1
ORM L39 .... 26 C2
STHP PR8 .... 14 C3
South Ter ORM L39 .... 30 D1
Southway SKEL WN8 .... 33 G5
Spa La BRSC L40 .... 32 A1
Spencer Pl
CHTN/BK (off Ashley Rd) PR9 .... 3 K4
Spencers Cft FMBY L37 .... 29 H4
WGNW/BIL/O WN5 .... 39 G5
Spinney Cl ORM L39 .... 30 C2
The Spinney FMBY L37 .... 29 G1
Spring Cl STHP PR8 .... 9 E5
Springfield Cl BRSC L40 .... 23 E5
FMBY L37 .... 28 C4
Spruce Wy FMBY L37 .... 28 C3
Spynners Cft FMBY L37 .... 24 C5
Square La BRSC L40 .... 23 H2
Squirrel Gn FMBY L37 .... 28 C1
Stafford Rd STHP PR8 .... 13 E4
Stafford St SKEL WN8 .... 32 C4
Stamford Rd CHTN/BK PR9 .... 13 F2
Standhouse La ORM L39 .... 30 B3
Stanlawe Rd FMBY L37 .... 28 C2
Stanley Av STHP PR8 .... 12 D3
Stanley Ct BRSC L40 .... 24 A5
Stanley Rd FMBY L37 .... 24 A5
SKEL WN8 .... 38 D1
Stanley St CHTN/BK PR9 .... 3 G3
Stanley Wy SKEL WN8 .... 32 D2
Stannanought Rd SKEL WN8 .... 34 A2
Statham Rd SKEL WN8 .... 32 D2
Statham Wy ORM L39 .... 30 D1
Station Ap BRSC L40 .... 23 F2

ORM* L39 .... 27 E5
Station Av WGNW/BIL/O WN5 .... 39 G3
Station Rd CHTN/BK PR9 .... 6 D2
ORM L39 .... 27 E4
STHP PR8 .... 19 E3
Staveley Av BRSC L40 .... 23 F3
Staveley Rd SKEL WN8 .... 32 D2
STHP PR8 .... 19 F4
The Stiles ORM L39 .... 26 D5
Stone Hall La SKEL WN8 .... 31 E4
Stoneleigh Cl STHP PR8 .... 19 E4
Stoney Brow SKEL WN8 .... 35 E3
Stourton St ORM L39 .... 19 E4
Straight Up La CHTN/BK PR9 .... 11 E2
Stratford Cl STHP PR8 .... 18 C2
Stretton Dr CHTN/BK PR9 .... 10 B2
Stub La BRSC L40 .... 22 B5
Sturgess Cl ORM L39 .... 27 E3
Suffolk Rd STHP PR8 .... 13 E5
Sugar Stubbs La CHTN/BK PR9 .... 7 G3
Sulby Cl STHP PR8 .... 12 D2
Summer St SKEL WN8 .... 33 E1
Sumner Rd STHP PR8 .... 12 F3
Sunbury Dr STHP PR8 .... 18 D4
Sunningdale Gdns FMBY L37 .... 29 E3
Sunnyfields ORM L39 .... 27 F5
Sunny Rd CHTN/BK PR9 .... 5 G5
Sunnyside STHP PR8 .... 12 D2
Sussex Rd CHTN/BK PR9 .... 3 K4
STHP PR8 ....
Sutton Rd FMBY L37 .... 29 E5
Swan Delph ORM L39 .... 30 B3
Swanpool La ORM L39 .... 30 B3
Sycamore Dr SKEL WN8 .... 32 D3
Sycamore Gv FMBY L37 .... 28 C5

T

Tadlow Cl FMBY L37 .... 28 C5
Talaton Cl CHTN/BK PR9 .... 5 G2
Talbot Dr STHP PR8 .... 3 G5
Talbot St STHP PR8 .... 3 F6
The Tamneys SKEL WN8 .... 33 E4
Tanfields SKEL WN8 .... 33 E4
Tanhouse Rd SKEL WN8 .... 34 A4
Tarleswood SKEL WN8 .... 33 E4
Tarleton Rd CHTN/BK PR9 .... 10 C2
Tarn Brow L39 .... 30 B3
Tarn Rd FMBY L37 .... 28 D3
Tarnside Rd WGNW/BIL/O WN5 .... 39 H2
Tarvin Cl CHTN/BK PR9 .... 6 B2
Tavistock Dr STHP PR8 .... 18 D2
Tawd Rd SKEL WN8 .... 33 H5
Taylor Av ORM L39 .... 32 B4
Taylor St SKEL WN8 .... 32 B4
Teal Cl ORM L39 .... 30 C2
Tedder Av CHTN/BK PR9 .... 10 C3
Tennyson Dr ORM L39 .... 26 C4
Teversham SKEL WN8 .... 33 E3
Tewkesbury SKEL * WN8 .... 33 E3
Thanet SKEL WN8 .... 33 E3
Thealby Cl SKEL WN8 .... 33 E3
Thirlmere Av CHTN/BK PR9 .... 29 G4
SKEL WN8 .... 39 E1
Thirlmere Ms
HTWN (off Thirlmere Rd) L38 .... 40 B3
Thirlmere Rd HTWN L38 .... 40 B3
Thirsk SKEL WN8 .... 32 D3
Thistleton Rd CHTN/BK PR9 .... 3 K2
Thompson Av ORM L39 .... 27 E5
Thornbeck Av HTWN L38 .... 40 A4
Thornbridge Av BRSC L40 .... 23 F4
Thornbury SKEL WN8 .... 33 E3
Thornhill ORM L39 .... 30 A4
Thornton Rd CHTN/BK PR9 .... 10 B3
Thornwood SKEL WN8 .... 33 E4
Thoroughgood Cl BRSC L40 .... 23 E5
Thorpe SKEL WN8 .... 33 E3
Three Pools CHTN/BK PR9 .... 6 A4
Three Tuns La FMBY L37 .... 29 F5
Threlfalls La CHTN/BK PR9 .... 5 F5
Thurcroft Dr SKEL WN8 .... 32 D3
Thursby Gv STHP PR8 .... 18 D5
Thurston SKEL WN8 .... 32 D3
Tilcroft SKEL WN8 .... 32 D3
Timms Cl FMBY L37 .... 29 F1
Timms La FMBY L37 .... 29 F1
Tinsley Av STHP PR8 .... 14 A2
Tinsley's La STHP PR8 .... 14 A3
Tintagel SKEL WN8 .... 32 C3
Tintern Dr FMBY L37 .... 29 H4
Tithebarn Rd STHP PR8 .... 9 H4
Tithebarn St SKEL * WN8 .... 39 E1
Tiverton Av SKEL WN8 .... 32 D3
Todd's La CHTN/BK PR9 .... 7 E1
Tollgate Rd BRSC L40 .... 22 C5
Tongbarn SKEL WN8 .... 32 D3
Tontine Rd SKEL WN8 .... 39 F2
Top Acre Rd SKEL WN8 .... 37 H1
Top Delph ORM L39 .... 27 F4
Torcross Cl CHTN/BK PR9 .... 5 G2
Totnes Dr CHTN/BK PR9 .... 5 G2
Tower Buildings
CHTN/BK (off Leicester St) PR9 .... 3 J1
Tower End FMBY L37 .... 28 C1
Tower Hl ORM L39 .... 27 F5

Index - featured places

 **Street by Street** QUESTIONNAIRE

Dear Atlas User
Your comments, opinions and recommendations are very important to us.
So please help us to improve our street atlases by taking a few minutes
to complete this simple questionnaire.

You do NOT need a stamp (unless posted outside the UK). If you do not want to remove this page from your street atlas, then photocopy it or write your answers on a plain sheet of paper.

Send to: The Editor, AA Street by Street, FREEPOST SCE 4598,
Basingstoke RG21 4GY

ABOUT THE ATLAS...

Which city/town/county did you buy?
_____

Are there any features of the atlas or mapping that you find particularly useful?
_____
_____
_____

Is there anything we could have done better?
_____
_____
_____

Why did you choose an AA Street by Street atlas?
_____
_____
_____

Did it meet your expectations?

Exceeded ☐　**Met all** ☐　**Met most** ☐　**Fell below** ☐

Please give your reasons
_____
_____
_____
_____

Where did you buy it?

For what purpose? (please tick all applicable)

To use in your own local area ☐   To use on business or at work ☐

Visiting a strange place ☐   In the car ☐   On foot ☐

Other (please state)

LOCAL KNOWLEDGE...

Local knowledge is invaluable. Whilst every attempt has been made to make the information contained in this atlas as accurate as possible, should you notice any inaccuracies, please detail them below (if necessary, use a blank piece of paper) or e-mail us at *streetbystreet@theAA.com*

ABOUT YOU...

Name (Mr/Mrs/Ms)

Address

                                                                    Postcode

Daytime tel no

E-mail address

Which age group are you in?

Under 25 ☐   **25-34** ☐   **35-44** ☐   **45-54** ☐   **55-64** ☐   **65+** ☐

Are you an AA member?   YES ☐   **NO** ☐

Do you have Internet access?   YES ☐   **NO** ☐

Thank you for taking the time to complete this questionnaire. Please send it to us as soon as possible, and remember, you do not need a stamp (unless posted outside the UK).

We may use information we hold about you to write to, or telephone, you about other products and services offered by us and our carefully selected partners. Information may be disclosed to other companies in the Centrica plc group (including those using British Gas, Scottish Gas, Goldfish and AA brands) but we can assure you that we not disclose it to third parties.

Tick box if you do NOT wish to hear about other products and services ☐   ML